ECHOES OF MY LOST TWIN

Owlthorpe Lane 1950

By: Alan John

Copyright ©2024 Alan John
All rights reserved.

Contents

Dedications	iv
Acknowledgements	v
About The Author	vi
Chapter 1: Tragic Birth	01
Chapter 2: Finding Guliemi	20
Chapter 3: Life In The Row	44
Chapter 4: Down The Mine	53
Chapter 5: Back To Guliemi Farm	62
Chapter 6: Where Is John?	69
Chapter 7: Two Worlds Into One	78
Chapter 8: The Homecoming	87
Chapter 9: Dog Wolf	91
Chapter 10: Guleimi	103
Chapter 11: Guliemi	113
Chapter 12: In Business	136

DEDICATIONS

I would like to dedicate this book to the most important people in my life - my family. To my wonderful parents, Arther and Louisa Booth, who have always supported and encouraged me in everything I do. To my two incredible daughters, Karen Elday and Paula Booth, who inspire me every day to be the best version of myself.

To my four grandchildren, Toni Ann, Danniele, Lauren, and Max, who fill my life with joy and laughter. And to my two greatgrandchildren, Lexie and Tristan.

Last but not least, I dedicate this book to my loving wife and rock, Janice. Thank you for being my partner in life and for always being there for me through thick and thin. This book would not have been possible without the love and support of all of you.

ACKNOWLEDGEMENTS

I would like to express my sincere gratitude to Karen Elday for her constant support and contribution to this project. Karen's willingness to spend time with me, discussing ideas and reading through my work, provided me with the motivation and confidence to keep going I am truly grateful for her time and efforts, which have helped make this book possible.

ABOUT THE AUTHOR

Alan Booth's journey started in a small village near Sheffield called Mosborough, where he was born in 1940. Only son of Arthur & Louisa, like them, he became and still is a well-respected and much-loved man of our community.

He has retired from engineering for 15 years now and has lived with Parkinson's disease for 15 years. He has been married to Janice for 59 years. She suffers from MS, and she has had this since she was 32 years old.

He used to own an engineering company, called Rother Valley Engineering, producing mining equipment employing around 20 people. The company had been doing well until the mines were closed down, so he went into Aerospace, making parts for Rolls Royce. His work included developing the F35 Joint strike fighter planes for the US army.

Alan has also played top-league squash for 30 years. When he retired, he returned to another passion of his: artwork, which was his hobby before he began playing squash. He has two lovely daughters, four grandchildren, and two great-grandchildren.

CHAPTER: 01
TRAGIC BIRTH

In the year 1940, nestled in a small northern English mining village, a tale unfolded that would forever haunt the hearts of its inhabitants. It began with the birth of twins Alan and John to a humble mining family.

As I entered into our second world, my primary thought was, where can I find John? Where's my twin?

He was there by my side, gasping for breath in this new world. I feared my lungs were bursting, a feeling of drowning in this strange, unfamiliar environment. We had been together as one for nine months in our first world. Now we're here. It's a strange, noisy world with lots of bright

flashing lights. As I tried to gather my senses, I had a feeling something was wrong. All at once, his body started to shake from head to toe as he turned his head, looking into my eyes, and he took his last breath. As he left this new world, a shining light exploded from him, spinning and pulsating, and his soul entered my body, and his thoughts were passed onto me. Now, we will always be as one now that we are one. So I was called Alan, John.

I woke up with a jolt. I'd been dreaming, or was it a dream? It was so realistic. Mum was shaking me, saying, "Alan, Alan, happy birthday! You're ten today. I think you were having a nightmare; you were fighting someone in your sleep, shouting and jumping about in bed. Why are you crying? Are you ok?"

"Yes," I said while shaking myself, trying to recollect my dream. I was sure I was in another real world – JOHN'S WORLD. Walking away, Mum shouted, "Time for school in an hour. Come down for breakfast when you're ready."

When Mum had gone, I started to come back to reality remembering who I am and where I am. Wow, that wasn't a dream. It was a premonition. John hadn't crossed my mind much in those ten years; Mum and Dad didn't talk about it at all, and I thought I had imagined it all. Quickly getting dressed, my thoughts returned to here and now.

Jack Hibbert was a nice, jolly, friendly chap who would do anything for us. He had a smallholding on the allotments with hens, and a cockerel that didn't go COCKA DOODLE DO, it just went DOODLE, DOODLE that made me smile every morning. He also had pigs, a goat, and a cow named Janet. When the cockerel started doodle doodling, it set off the cow to MOO MOO. To finish off his mini farm, he had NODDY, his horse that did the ploughing, led by Jack's oldest son TOM, a 16-year-old big strong, sturdy lad just like his horse.

As I sat eating my breakfast, eggs on toast, I remembered we got the eggs from Jack's mini farm. Some foods were still on ration in 1950, five years after the end of WWII. But we managed because Dad swapped bags of coal for food with Jack. Finishing my breakfast, I glanced out of the window and spotted Ray waiting outside for me to walk down to school together. Slamming the door behind me, I shouted, "Hi Ray, let's go amigo!" Ray and I were walking towards the Hibbert house when Tom passed us with Noddy. Both Tom and the horse were soaked with sweat. Then, to our amazement, Tom led Noddy into the house and filled the sink with water. Noddy drank from it eagerly. I glanced at Ray, and we both held out our arms and shrugged our shoulders. Ray stuttered, "I..I.. I've seen it all now, Al!"

We set off down Owlthorpe Lane. Halfway down the lane, we could hear a whimpering coming from the long grass. We looked at each other and decided to go into the field to investigate. As we got closer, we spotted a long-haired, reddish-brown dog. Carefully approaching the dog, we sensed it was friendly because of its sad 'come and help me' eyes. We soon discovered she was called Sally.

Carefully stroking her we could feel lumps and bumps. She looked as though she had been beaten. While we examined her, she was shaking with fear. "Wha? What do we do now?" stuttered Ray.

Well, we have to go to school, although it's the last day before the summer holidays we'll be done if we miss it!" I replied, and Ray started to walk away. Sally struggled and stood up to follow us.

"We can't leave her," I pleaded with him.

with fear. "Wha? What do we do now?" stuttered Ray.

Well, we have to go to school, although it's the last day before the summer holidays we'll be done if we miss it!" I replied, and Ray started to walk away. Sally struggled and stood up to follow us.

"We can't leave her," I pleaded with him.

"Ok, ok... le..le..let's have a think. We can get her a drink from the sawmill. Let's walk across and see if she follows." Replied Ray.

Sure enough, as we walked across to the sawmill, she limped along after us. We could hear the loud whizzing sound as Harry (Staton) was busy sawing timber up to all shapes and sizes.

was busy sawing timber up to all shapes and sizes.

"Morning lads, what can I do for you two scallywags?"

" He asked when he saw us.

"We've found this dog. She looks in a bad condition." I explained, "Can we get her a drink,Harry?" I tried to shout above the noise, just as he stopped the saw.

"Yes, sure, over there in the cabin. What are you going to do with her?" Harry replied.

"Dddd... don't know," Ray chimed in. We are supposed to be going to school. HARRY bent over, gave Sally a drink, and then went over to his snap box. He opened up a sandwich he had in there, took a couple of sausages from the sandwich, and threw them down for Sally, who hungrily gobbled them down.

"Wow," I said. She was starving. Tapping Ray on the shoulder, I said, "Jack Hibberts got an empty pigsty; we could put her in there until she gets better."

"What about school?" Ray asked with his arms crossed, waiting for an answer.

"We can go around the back way across the field

through the woods and into the allotment without being seen," I replied.

Right, right," Ray said, "That's a good plan. Let's go, Sally!"

Setting off from the sawmill, we could see Sally was struggling and limping, so we took turns carrying her across the field; we had a rest on the hill above the wood, where we all sat down for a breather. In the distance, coming out of the woods, was a boy with a red scarf on. He looked about 12„ slightly older than us. He looked a bit of a scruff with matted black hair and clothes covered in oil; when he spotted Sally, he shouted, "There you are, come here, you bitch!" he was waving a large stick, as he said, "You all get some of this."

I looked at Ray nervously, thinking, what do we do now, as he approached angrily, waving the stick around. I felt an unusual happening stirring inside of me, and I could sense John's presence for the first time since our birth. It was as though someone had taken over my body; I felt a sense that it was John taking control, as I jumped up, snatching the stick from him, shouting, "You're not taking her anywhere, you bully!"

He was just about to retaliate when Ray stood up and stepped forward. The boy hesitated and turned around, running off and shouting, "I'll be back for her." Walking up to the allotments, all three of us reached the pigsty.

In the pigsty, she playfully kept rolling around in straw. It was still quite early, so we didn't want to be seen because we were supposed to be at school. We snuggled down in the straw with Sally and fell asleep. We were suddenly awoken by a loud voice,

"HOY, what are you doing in here? Let's have you out, like now."

Rubbing our eyes and shaking head to toe, we woke up to see Tom Hibbert standing over us. He looked like a giant from where we were lying. Ray stuttered out, "Sss..sorry T..t..Tom, we've found an injured dog and..." He started telling him the full story.

"HOY, what are you doing in here? Let's have you out, like now."

Rubbing our eyes and shaking head to toe, we woke up to see Tom Hibbert standing over us. He looked like a giant from where we were lying. Ray stuttered out, "Sss..sorry T..t..Tom, we've found an injured dog and..." He started telling him the full story.

After hearing Ray out, Tom's attitude changed to one of pure sympathy, and he bent down to check her over. Sally gave him a nervous growl, sitting up and showing her teeth. Tom stepped back as he could see fear in her eyes but also a glimmer of hope as she realised he meant her no harm. Tom slowly offered an extended Hi hand as a gesture of trust, and Sally hesitated for a moment before sniffing Tom's hand, then gently giving it a lick. Sensing the dog's vulnerability, Tom spoke in a soft, gentle, reassuring voice, "Hey there, girl! It looks as though you've been in the wars. Now you wait there!" Tom said and disappeared. Ray and I looked at each other and shrugged, now we're for it, I said. Tom returned, and we could hear his footsteps, dreading what the consequences were going to be. He came in with a bowl of water, some dog food, and some ointment to rub on Sally. He bent and some ointment to rub on Sally. He bent over to us and whispered,

"I think we better keep this to ourselves, don't you think?" Ray and I nodded in agreement. He then put down the food, water, and ointment and walked out. Ray looked at me and gave a nervous smile.

We came out of the stay as though we had returned from school. I opened our door and shouted, "I'm back from school, Mum." Sitting down in the yard, Ray pulled out a bag of Marbles. He gave me half, and as we started to play, he produced half a dozen larger marbles called Pottys. "They are brilliant," I said, "Can I go and show them to Dad and see if he will get me some?" Dad was sitting at the table. I walked up to him and showed him the potty, "Dad, will you get me some of these?" I asked.

"We will see," he replied. "Now go out and play. Don't put them in your mouth."

Slamming the door behind me, I got confused and put a potty in my mouth. And accidentally swallowed it, too. Panicking, I ran back inside the house, "Dad, I've swallowed one."

"Oh dear," Up he jumped, running out of the house shouting "Jack, Jack."

Jack climbed into his lorry, and Dad got in the front seat. As we set off, we could hear clucking and quacking. I turned around and saw several cages with ducks, hens, and chickens. "We're not taking them, are we, Jack?" Dad enquired.

"We've no choice. It's an emergency," Jack replied as he drove off in the old lorry, which rattled and creaked with the sound of ducks and hens clucking and quacking.

As we approached the hospital, the lorry suddenly jolted up in the air as if it had hit a brick or something. The birds in the cages got quite alarmed and started making even more noise. When we got to the accident and emergency department, I was shown to a cubicle and waited for the doctor to examine me. After the examination, the doctor sent me for an X-ray, and I began to feel really stressed while waiting for the results.

Finally, the doctor came back with a smile on his face and told me that everything was okay. The object would pass through my body naturally, and I could go home. As we left the A and E, we were greeted with an unexpected sight. The area outside the hospital was full of ducks, hens, and chickens, with several staff members trying to round them up. I couldn't help but smile, but Jack went berserk, running around and trying to catch his chickens and ducks. Eventually, he caught them all, but it was like something out of a Laurel and Hardy film.

We got back home, and I linked up with Ray, and we checked on Sally, fed her, watered her and bedded her down for the night. I was quite pleased with her. She seemed more mobile and relaxed.

During the night, Sally started howling and woke me up. I started to get wound up, thinking that if she woke everybody up, they would find her. So, I dressed and went outside across to the pigsty with some bread and water. I laid down with Sally to calm her down. All of a sudden, I could hear my mum shouting to me, "Alan! Alan!"

So, I ran out of the pigsty towards Mum and held my arms out as though I was sleepwalking. "Where am I mum?"

"What are you doing out here?" She shouted.

"I don't know how I got here. I was asleep." Mum looked at me, frightened. She led me back to the house and to bed, where she refused to leave until I was asleep.

By now, it was a deep, deep, mysterious, puzzling sleep, but all so real. I was convinced that it was happening somewhere, but where were we?

The early morning mist disguised the features of this strange province. John and I were bound together by apprehensive trepidation. It was so real that I could feel it, smell it, and touch it. John looked agitated he was trembling from head to toe.

Looking around, I had a feeling we were being followed. Slowly, as the mist started to lift, the surroundings became more visible. It was a very busy market town with no cars, lorries or buses – just horses and carts. The people were wearing odd clothes, and the men had long hair. They were all looking at John and I. We, too, had long hair and unfamiliar clothes. As the mist were all looking at John and I. We, too, had long hair and unfamiliar clothes. As the mist cleared, buildings started to appear out of nowhere. This place felt like an alien world, with market stalls, cobbled streets and a fowl odour, as there were no drains, making everything dingy.

Looking up, I saw a twisted church spire. Somewhere in the distance, I could hear a doodle, doodle that repeated several times, getting louder and followed by a moo, moo. Rubbing my eyes in shock, I sat up and realised that I was back in Owl Thorpe Lane.

Jack's animal wake-up call had brought me back to reality from my other world.

As I was shovelling breakfast down as fast as possible to go and see Sally, there was a loud knock at the door. Dad stood up. I felt nervous and opened the door, and it was a boy with a red scarf.

"I've come for my dog. Your son has my dog." He told my Dad.

"ALAN!" My Dad shouted, "What's he on about?" I nervously explained the situation to him, and he asked me to take him to this dog.

"It's in Mr Hibbert's pigsty.." I stuttered, sounding like my mate, Ray.
"Come on, let's go."

On reaching the pigsty, Dad looked at Sally and asked me to give the boy his dog back. From the back of my mind, recalling my dream about John, came a united response. As though John was here backing me up, I said, "I won't. He's a bully and beats her up." Then, cringing and expecting a backlash, I waited for a response from my dad, who stared at me intensely for a few seconds that felt like hours.

Finally, he turned to the boy and asked, "How much

did the dog cost you?"

The boy responded, "£2."

Surprisingly, my dad pulled out two crispy pound notes from his pocket, gave them to the boy, and said, "Now be off with you." The boy gave a little grin and skipped away as though he had won the pools.

Then, my dad looked at me, rubbed my head, and said, "Well done, lad. You were right. Bring Sally into the house, and we will give her a big bone."

And that's how Sally became a part of our lives.

CHAPTER: 02
FINDING GULIEMI

Back in the house with Sally, Mum scratched her head and asked, "Where's the dog from?"

"It's my new dog," I said and Dad began to explain as I dashed out with Sally to share the good news with Ray. Several of the Hibberts' youngsters and Ray were playing in the yard when they noticed Sally. We were soon surrounded by kids of all ages and sizes.

"Let's take her for a walk, Ray," I suggested.

"Yes, if she's okay," Ray responded.

So off we went on a new adventure, both excited to have a new friend. We walked down the path that runs alongside the allotments and onto the field that leads to the woods.

Once on the field, Sally ran around chasing birds, leaves, or anything that moved. We approached the woods, called Inglee, an old Saxon name that meant "hanging Lee,"

The first thing that we noticed was the wonderful

carpet of bluebells spreading as far as the eye could see. Sally was busy chasing squirrels up the trees. Partway down, an orange stream emerged out of nowhere. It flowed from the drift mine over the hill. We eagerly followed the orange water to see where it would lead. Ray nervously stuttered, "Shall we go back now? We might get lost. I don't recognise this area." As Ray spoke, we heard a chanting noise in the distance as though it was a foreign language. Ray and I looked at each other and shrugged our shoulders, but Sally was intrigued. She wanted to know more and shuffled up closer to the sounds. She cocked her head to one side as if puzzled but kept on sneaking up nearer to the chanting. Ray and I carefully and quietly followed.

As we looked through the dense bush, an amazing sight caught our eye. We could see flickering flames from a campfire through the bushes. The flames were dancing in all the colours of the rainbow. There was a man, who looked like a weird tramp, sitting around the fire. The fire lit up the scene, and the man was surrounded by animals and birds that seemed to adore him as though he were their master. We watched quietly in silence until Sally,

upon seeing the badger and foxes, started growling at them.

She couldn't hold back any longer and ran over to them. The man, upon seeing Sally, wasn't the slightest bit perturbed. He put his hand up and said, "Hello, girl, what are you doing here?" At that point, Sally stopped dead in her tracks as if she had frozen in time. We stood up, tranced and fixed on what had happened. On seeing us, the man said in a soft, gentle manner, "Come on over, boys."

Cautiously, we inched towards him not knowing what and why he was up to. "Sit down, lads," he said as he stoked the fire and then added more wood.

As we approached him, Ray enquired, "Do you live here?"

"I have lived here many years," he answered, "but sometimes, I'm not of this world," he said with a strange look on his face, looking up to the heavens. "I have been sent back to help my friends here," he said with his arms outstretched, pointing at the animals. I returned when things started to get out of hand.

"How long have you been coming here?" I asked.

"Well, over 200 years." He calmly replied. Ray gave me a nervous half-smile.

He then began talking about how his friends, the animals, come to him for help whenever they are ill while pointing to a badger that was chewing on a root. I looked at him, puzzled, as the badger chewed greedily on the root.

"What's that then, sir?" I asked in wonderment.

"Don't call me sir. My name is GULIEMI. And it's liquorice root if you know where to find it; it has magical properties."

Guliemi then turned to me and said, "Are you one of the twins?"
I looked at him with a puzzled look on my face. "How do you know I was a twin?" I asked.

"Was? What do you mean WAS?" He shouted.

"Yes, because... I am Alan, and John died." My voice broke. It was now really affecting me emotionally. My voice was barely a whisper.

"Oh no, he didn't." He retorted, "I've been waiting for you two for a hundred years, and it's not what is written in destiny. So you better find him. I can feel his presence in this world." Then, standing up straight as if he was about to declare something major, he said, "Alan, I have something for you, but it will only start to have an effect when you find John."

He went inside his den and came out with a scroll. Passing it to me, he said, "For reasons you will later discover you will eventually inherit my gifts and my properties." He stood up and walked into his den once again, his image disappearing in the darkness. At the same time, the animals and birds slowly walked away. Strangely, Ray, Sally and I stood up in unison and started walking away.

On the way back, I whispered to Ray, "Let's get back home. I feel a bit weird and dizzy." I opened up the scroll he gave me.

Walking back home up from the woods I spotted several wasps entering a small hole in the banking. I wondered what's in there. Out of curiosity, I picked a stick up and gave it a poke. Within a minute, thousands of wasps came out of the hole. They were angry – no, mad. In fact, they weren't just mad; they were furious; they went ballistic. Sally was the first off-the-mark zoom.

Like a flash, she was out of there not looking back

as she disappeared into the distance.

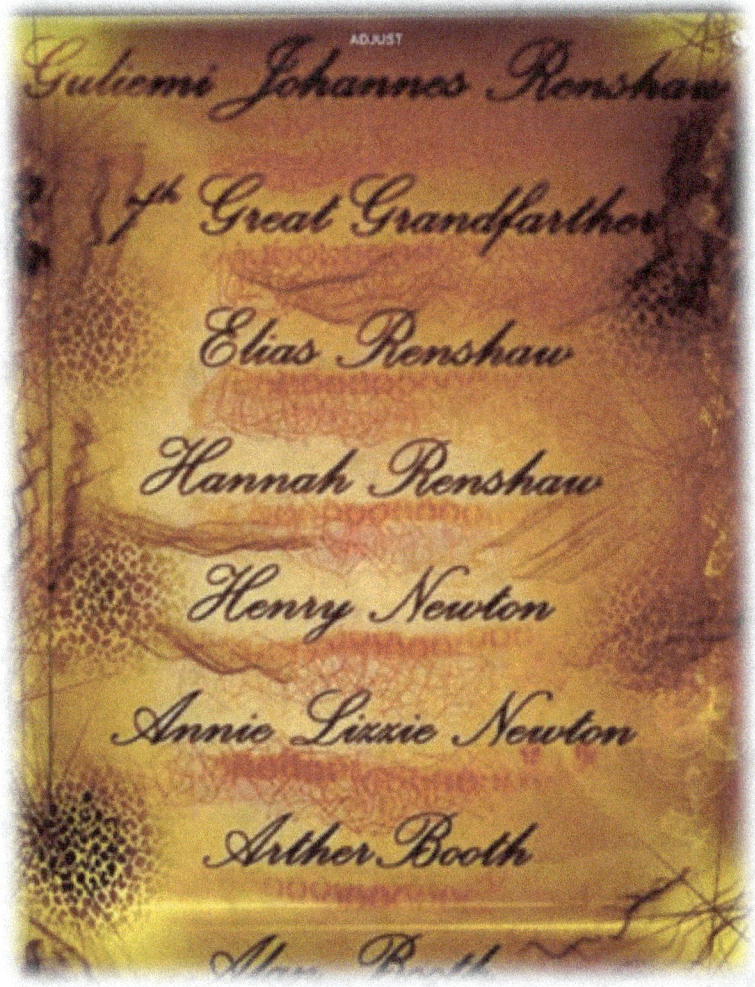

Ray and I were shocked until we heard the loud buzzing noise of the wasps. We bolted after Sally, with thousands of wasps in the chase. We reached the allotments near the cottages where Tom was ploughing with Noddy. Luckily for us, the wasps changed their direction and started buzzing after Tom and Noddy. The horse was so alarmed that it bolted, dragging Tom across the allotment into the hedge. Noddy kept on running, leaving Tom stuck in the hedge with the wasps gradually dispersing and disappearing. Tom sat up in the hedge, looking stunned as if he had been hit by a bomb.

The next day, I overheard my dad chatting with Jack. He mentioned that his horse was ill. Suddenly, a thought popped into my mind as if John whispered to me softly, "I have an idea." Sally and I went to pick up Ray, and while walking down to the woods, I explained our plan. We were going to heal Mr Hibbert's horse by using something from Guliemi.

As we followed the orange water again, we retraced our steps of yesterday and found the spot where Guliemi camped, Sally ran over to the badgers now as they were old friends. Guliemi was just coming out of his den when he lifted his hand to beckon us over. After chatting for a while, I explained what the problem was. He said there are four sticks of liquorice root; give the horse three sticks, and it should be better in a matter of hours. If not, give it the one stick the next day, and that should do the trick. Walking back, we were so excited we ran back home, eager to find out if Guliemi was correct.

Getting on to the allotment, we found Noddy in the stable. Well, you couldn't call it a stable; it was just a shed. We went over to him, and there was no one around so we gave him all three sticks of liquorice root. After five minutes, he started running round in circles like a cat chasing its tail, then shaking his head back and forth. We started to get worried as he was neighing and snorting; it felt like he was going berserk. Noddy went over to the water trough and started to lap it up as though he was on fire. "What have we done?" I thought. He then did some stretching and blowing out of his mouth. We were scared and ran away, keeping out of his way until morning. When Jack knocked on the door, I became afraid and called out to my dad. Arthur heard and went to see what was happening. Jack told us that there was something miraculous about Noddy and that he was now healthy and full of energy. It felt like someone was watching over me, and Arthur was beaming with joy.

"Ray, Ray!" I ran over to him. "We've sorted it out. The horse is okay now. Let's go and thank Guliemi." Running excitedly past the allotment, across two fields, and down to the orange waters, we finally reached the spot where Guliemi had camped. But there was nothing there, as though he had never existed. No scorched earth where the fire had been. No den, no badgers, trees, and bushes that had never been there. We scratched our heads in disbelief. Had we dreamt this? Had we imagined it? Was it a dream or a fantasy? As we walked away, I put my hand in my pocket and found the one liquorice root we had left. So it was all real. Or was it? Only you can decide for yourself.

I was disturbed during the night by the scuffling sounds coming from under the floorboards. I lay awake for what seemed like an eternity while the sounds continued – scuffle, scuffle, scratch, scratch. There was no light in my bedroom, so I turned my torch on and saw four eyes staring at me.

What was it? Was it a monster? Or a ghost? What

kind of creature has four eyes? I held my breath. My eyes went wide as dinner plates, my mouth dropped open, and my torch lit up as I let out an enormous scream. I was about to slink down the bed in fear when John came into my head shouting, "Sally, go and get them!" Two rats stared me out as Sally and the rats ran around the bedroom, knocking things over and creating chaos. Mum eventually came into the room to calm me down. She whispered that we had to put up with it until we could move. I looked at my clock and saw that it was 3:30 AM. I knew that I needed to get up soon to help my dad get ready for his double shift at Westhorpe Mine. He had to start at 6:00 AM and had a few hours to walk there. He and his coworkers would stay at Grammar Wallers for the night.

It was about dinnertime when we set off for grammar wallers. Walking from Owlthorpe Lane to British Oak Row was about half a mile. As Mum, Sally, and I got closer, I could see that the funfair had arrived in the field opposite. They were just setting up. "Mum, can we go to the fair later?" I pleaded.

Mum was the second youngest of 12 kids, all brought

brought up at number 9. Grammar had a dog called Prince, a fox terrier with one ear stuck up and one ear bent, which my dad called "Odd Tabs". Some of Mum's brothers and sisters lived on the row, so it was a small community of its own.

It was finally time for the fair. The fair opened at 5 PM, so we went early before it got busy. My friend Sally and I walked around and saw a boy with a red scarf grinning at me on the big Walzer roundabout. I continued to walk around nervously and watched a man attempting to knock coconuts off a post at a stall. When I looked down at the dog lead, Sally was no longer there. I ran around shouting "Sally, Sally," but she had disappeared. After an hour of desperate attempts, we finally started to walk off the fairground. The red scarf boy appeared again, staring at me with an enormous grin on his face. We gave up and reluctantly returned to number nine. My heart was shattered.

My mom went to bed and helped me fall asleep, but I couldn't relax. In the middle of the night, John barged into my thoughts, urgently yelling at me to wake up because he knew where Sally was. He claimed he had just seen her tied up under a caravan. Hastily, I got dressed and stealthily left my house, equipped with my dog leash and flashlight. As I cautiously made my way across the road, the fairground was eerily silent except for the occasional chirping of birds. Using only my torch for light, I found Sally tied up under a caravan after following the sound of a dog whining. I nervously untied her and slipped her on the lead. My heart was racing away as I tiptoed away out of the fairground across the road and back into number nine. We jumped on the settee with Sally licking me all over with gratitude. We got covered up and went into lovely slumber.

Mum was first up at number 9, and she came into the room while I was just waking up. "Morning, Alan. How are you, love? We will go and look for Sally again. Don't worry, I'm sure we will find her." Just as she finished speaking, Sally popped her head out of the blanket. "Where has she come from?" Mum shouted.

"Er, Er…" I was stuttering again. "I heard a scratching at the door," I lied. "OH, I'm so relieved, Mum."

We had some nice cheese on toast for breakfast, it was home-baked bread that was done fresh every day. "Mum, where does the orange water come from?" I asked.

"It is pumped from the drift mine across the road to stop the mine flooding," I was told.

"Why is it orange, then?" I questioned.

"It's rich in iron," she replied. "If you are interested, I have a book on old Mosborough."

"Yes, please," I quickly replied.

Grammar got up, went over to the dresser, and came back with this old tatty book - it looked a hundred years old! "You can borrow it, but I want it back. I've had it for years." She said.

'I can tell,' I thought. As everything went quiet, I overheard Mum talking to Grammar about a vacant house in row Number 17. Mum also explained about the rats up at Owlthorpe. She was interested.

•••

After breakfast, we went back up to Owlthorpe Lane because Dad was on his way back from the mine, and Mum wanted to prepare a meal for him. We waved to Knucky at the sawmill and bumped into Mrs Hibberts, who was complaining that they had no coal for the fire. Mum said I would have a word with Arthur and Sally was running around chasing anything that moved. We arrived home and I discovered Ray had gone out for the afternoon, so I settled down to read some of the Grammar's old scraggy book. I came across Chapter One of "Tales of Mosborough Hall," which looked interesting, so I sat down to read it. Then, I moved on to Chapter Two, "Geilami, the Mystery Man of the Woods." The word "Geilami" caught my attention, and I was immediately drawn into the story. The book explained that a tramp-like man had been seen around the Inglee since 1821 and was followed by groups of animals. He was believed to be a mystical animal healer, WOW. I couldn't wait to see Ray and show him this.

It was the next morning that Dad announced that he had l couple of days off and that we were going for a picnic. So, Mum got bits and bobs together.

We hadn't got much, but it was a nice day, so why not? I still hadn't spoken to Ray about you know who. Dad said just before we go, I have to take two sacks of coal to Jack as they have no fire. I went with Dad to the coal shed and then to the Hibberts with two sacks of coal. When we got back, Mum was all packed, and off we went down the path beside the allotment, across one field, and we found a nice spot at one of the fields overlooking the woods. It was a nice sunny day.

Mum unpacked the blanket to put the food while Dad and I enjoyed some homemade pork pies for starters and Carnation cream sandwiches, washed down with gallons of dandelion and burdock pop. Meanwhile, Sally was busy chasing squirrels away from the food. Suddenly, we all noticed a ghostly, misty figure appear in the field next to the woods. He was almost transparent. Sally ran to the edge of the field, barking at the figure as he walked across the field towards the woods. His opacity grew clearer and more visible. As if we had waved a magic wand, he disappeared into the woods. We all looked at each other, not knowing what to say. Mum looked at Dad and asked, "What happened there? Did I imagine that? Did you see that old man who seemed to come out of thin air?" while scratching her head. I thought to myself, "Keep your mouth shut, Alan," but it looked like Guliemi to me. Yes, that was very strange, I muttered. Mum started packing our bags, and Sally kept on running back to the spot and barking. She wouldn't let it be, and we had to put her on the lead to get her home.

"Come on, Alan, we are moving tomorrow down to British Oak Row. Get your things packed in that box. We are nearly packed, and off we'll go tomorrow to 17 Mosborough." So, I started packing my books with my mind still on my flashbacks what Mum calls daydreaming. Going through my books, I picked up the old book Grammar Waller lent me three years ago, Tales of old Mosborough; I never finished that second chapter Guliemi Renshaw, reading on my eyes popped out when it said {in 1822, Guleimi Renshaw had twin boys named ALAN and JOHN}, born in Chesterfield, Derbyshire. As I was reading, my Dad popped into the room, snatched the book from my hands, and threw it into the box. Then, taking the box downstairs, he said, "Go to sleep. We have a long day tomorrow." As soon as I closed my eyes, I was drifting back.

I was lying awake when a flashback hit me. In the memory, John and I were back in our old town, running from an unknown threat. As we became more aware of our surroundings, we headed towards our home, and things started to make sense. We were on a country lane, and as we approached our farm, which had a signpost reading "GULEIMI FARM," we breathed a sigh of relief, feeling safe again. However, we couldn't remember who or what we were running from, leaving us perplexed. First, we crossed the cow field, and the cows all started nodding their heads and came over, licking and rubbing their bodies against us like pet dogs;

Then, we scrambled out of the cow field and making way towards the farmhouse. The sheep did the same, nodding their heads and rubbing us up in a gentle, friendly manner. We looked at each other and shrugged. Apparently, for some reason, we were very popular with the animals. On entering the farm area, a mist suddenly surrounded us, and as the mist got thicker and thicker, I started to flounder. Where was I? Then, as the mist lifted, I was back in the row.

The next morning, Jack pulled up with his lorry to move us to the Row. Sally, like a flash of lightning, jumped straight on the back of the lorry, and there was no way that we were going without her. Dad had to pack the lorry around her, so after a couple of hours of packing the lorry, we went off down to the Row. It was less than a mile down to the Row but only a few hundred yards down the lane. There was a loud bang from under the bonnet and up went a large black puff of smoke from the engine as the lorry collapsed like a huge animal that had just had enough. After twenty minutes, Jack came back with the verdict. Looked like a minister giving the last rites, head down, hands clasped together solemnly announcing the gearbox had blown. So here we were, stuck at the bottom of the lane halfway into the road with the cars pipping because we were blocking the traffic. Jack and Dad stood looking at each other, scratching their heads, and Mum and I looked bewildered. At last, we had an idea: fetch Noddy his horse. It must have been all of twenty minutes but spent like hours. Jack, with his son Tom, came back with Noddy, tied him to the lorry with a bull rope, and started to pull the lorry down the Row. By now, we had created a large audience of people who stood there laughing, and I felt like a fool. At last, we entered the Row with a large cheer from the neighbours, and we were finally home. It did feel like home.

CHAPTER: 03
LIFE IN THE ROW

Life in the Row was good. We had an allotment with an apple tree. My granddad gave me an old pigeon coat, and my dad got us six hens. So, we had 3 or 4 eggs a day. In the British Oak pub lived my Mum's sister, Aunt Mary, and my two cousins, Willis and Stuart. At number nine lived grandma and granddad Waller, who had a dog called Prince. Dad called him odd tabs because he had one ear bent as usual and one ear stuck up. On the first morning, I got a glimpse of not my healing powers but John's. While we were down at number nine, odd tabs went into a kind of fit, and everyone was running around in circles. John said to me, "Stand back, Alan," as he took control of the situation, bent down, and laid his hands on odd tabs. Within minutes, he was back to normal. While nobody thought much of it, I knew it was John, not me, who had the gift of healing.

My uncle Urn, mum's brother, who lived at 21, called to see us and asked if we would save all potato peelings and veg to make pig swill as he had bought two baby pigs, and they were only two months old.

"Can I come and have a look?" I asked.

"Yes, teacake," he replied. Teacake was his nickname for me, and I don't know why, so I called him Pieclet. Just as we were coming out of our tiny yard, this massive cockerel came out of nowhere, flying across the big yard and going straight for me. Piecet picked up a sweeping brush and gave it a wack that any golfer would be proud of. He was running back for more when Sally came out of the house barking and chased it back into the pen. Turned out it was next door, Mr Bounds, and it had a loose tile. So, we eventually got to see the piglets. Pieclet said they were two sows, so I called them Doris and Doreen.

As I walked back to number 17, I began to feel hot, sweaty, and feverish. Sweat was pouring out of me, so I went to lie down on the settee. My mum came over and put a hand on my forehead. She said I had a temperature and made a cold compress to cool me down. As this was happening, I felt my body rising and floating in the air until I reached the ceiling. Looking down on myself laid on the settee with my mum mopping my brow. I was disoriented and confused, and my world was spinning in tremors. The next thing I realised was

John and I were walking together to Guileimu farm.

As we walked into the farm cottage, John was still shaking when he thought about the incident when two men attacked him and tried to snatch him as he was on his own.

We told Dad, and he said you don't over-dramatize things. You have a fanciful nature; why would anyone want to kidnap you? Forget it. He said, anyway, I've got a job for you two. The milk needs to be taken to the market in Chesterfield tomorrow morning. You'll have to leave by five to get there early for six.

So, we were up at four, had a couple of fried eggs for breakfast, and then loaded the milk onto the wagon. We fetched the horses from the stable and coupled them up, and it was just coming light. The animals on the farm were shuffling about, waking up cows, sheep, hens, and pigs; I think they were getting hungry, so there was plenty for Dad to do while we were away in Chesterfield. The two sheepdogs (Bill and Ben) were sitting silently with their chins on their paws, waiting for their workout today. Dad and farmhand Knucky, a quiet, unassuming, friendly fellow, was getting ready to take out to Bill and Ben.

We set off slowly with all the milk onboard swishing about in the churns, slowly up the lane heading for Chesterfield market. We had a few stops on the way to different customers. Entering the town, it was busy even at six o'clock. Just about ten minutes to the market, a dog suddenly ran out barking at the horses. They jumped back in panic, and I lost my balance and fell to the ground head-first. I must have been out for ten minutes or so because as I sat up, feeling the lump on my head, there was a large crowd and about a hundred cats.

One of the milk churns had fallen off in the mayhem, cats coming from everywhere, attacking the milk in a frenzy as though it was cats' Christmas. This turned the horses to trepidation mode, and they took off at a rocket pace with John still on board, parting the crowds like Moses with the Red Sea, going about a hundred yards, then stopping dead in their tracks as some kind of miracle had happened. John jumped off the wagon and looked under the wheels. He put his hands to his head and gasped in horror as he pulled the dog out from under the wheels; the dog lifted up its head, gave a last gasp, and collapsed. The people around put their hands to their heads in horror. John put one hand under the dog's head and waved the other over the head moving back and forwards as though he was about to commit a miracle which is exactly what he did. The dog suddenly sat up, licked John's hand, and scuppered off into the distance. I felt the lump on my head, it was quite large. Slowly, my head started to go vague and my vision blurred. I began feeling drowsy and before I knew it, I flopped down on the road and everything went black.

When I came around I was on the back of the milk

wagon, rattling amongst the churns. John shouted, "Wake up, Alan! We still have got to deliver this milk. Dad's got a lot of money tied up in this, if we don't deliver we will lose the contract to another farm."

As we turned the corner to the market; the market manager was livid when he saw John. Then John, remembering what happened the last time they met, started shaking from head to foot. Charlie, the Market Manager, shouted, "Come here, you Casanova!" He grabbed John by the collar of his shirt, pulled him off the wagon grabbed him by the throat. With a screwed-up grimace on his face, Charlie put his nose up to John and raged, "Next time I see you with my daughter, I will give you a pasting you won't forget. Now unload that milk – you're half an hour late!" We quickly unloaded the milk and drove back to the farm. John turned to me and asked, "Why didn't you tell him it was you, Al?"

"Not bloody likely," I said. Climbing into the back of the wagon, I told John, "My head is spinning. I'll have a sleep while you drive back." Holding the lump on my head, I was away in seconds.

As I awoke, Sally was on the sofa with me, and I was drenched in sweat. Recovering from the strange fever-like symptoms I had a couple of hours ago, it did seem like days ago. Mum came in from the kitchen. "Are you feeling better? Alan, you had a dreadful temperature earlier," she said.

"I had a strange experience," I told Mum as we returned to the Row at Mosborough. "It wasn't a dream, and it felt so real. I dreamt that John and I were together." As I sat up, I held my head and felt a large lump.

"Where did you get that lump, Alan? I only left you

for a minute," my mum asked.

"I don't know, Mum. I just woke up with it," I replied. "That's worrying," my mum said.

"You should go to the doctor and have it looked at."

CHAPTER: 04

DOWN THE MINE

"Well, Dad and I are going to the pub tonight, so you will be on your own for an hour or two-" Just as Mum was speaking, Willis came in (my cousin from British Oak pub).

While my parents were getting ready for the pub, I asked Willis, "Do you want to stop in with me, and we will do some chips?" I knew that Willis would not refuse a meal. My dad always said he could make a sandwich out of a tomato seed. Before going to the pub, dad always went to the coal shed and picked up the biggest lump of coal, put it in a bag, picked a table near the fire, and threw on the lump that would last all night. When we got rid of them, we cut up some chips, put them on the chip pan, and got the chips going while we were listening to the ovalities on the radio. Luxemburg was on in the background when Sally started barking in the kitchen. We ran in and saw massive flames coming from the chip pan. So, what do you do in a fire? Well, it's obvious - you pour water on it. Anyone knows that. I had never heard a bomb go off before, but I did that day. BANG, WOOSH, KAPOW! Willis and I were running around like LOURAL AND HARDY on fast forward. Willis ran down to the pub to tell my mum while I tried to put out the fire. The shelves above the cooker were decorated with fancy paper, and it caught fire. By the time they returned, I had managed to put the fire out. Granted, the kitchen looked like a bomb zone with a flood, but I had done an excellent job of putting out the fire. However, my dad went berserk. I thought I'd done a great job.

After a few days in the Row, I made many friends besides my cousins Willis and Stuart (Dickie). There was Tup, Keith, and his brother Tich. We were planning the biggest bonfire in the orchard of the British Oak. It was Sunday, so we planned a raid on the drift mine across the road, Pit props for the bonfire. While everyone was at church and chapel, we went down Bramall's lane and up to the drift mine. There were gooseberry bushes on the way up, so we made a short stop for lunch. The drift mine was deserted as we were looking around for pit props. Stuart (Dickie) was climbing in the coal tubs, messing around, when there we heard a rumbling sound. It was like the loudest thunder. I looked up and realised that the tub had loosened. Dickie was heading down into the drift mine. You can't put into words the look of fear on our faces. Rumble. Rumble. Rumble. The tub went down into the mine with a loud bang and crash. We stood there in horror, completely silent. Panic set in as we realised we had no torch to look for him. Tup suggested that there was a lamp nearby that we could light up, and we could use it to search for Dickie. After several attempts, we finally got the lamp working and agreed that the two of us should go and look while the others waited with bated breath. Willis insisted on going down, but the rest of us voted for me. So, Willis and I, with the miner's lamp, nervously started down the drift mine, with Sally following closely behind. When we had gone about a hundred yards deep, there was a smaller passage, but the Tub lines carried onto the large one. We stopped and looked down the small passage, Sally was whimpering and whining and we saw two large, yellow eyes appear in the distance. I heard John speak to me in my head,

saying its squeaky bum time. We all stepped back

in unison as an enormous roar came out of the smaller passage. A large creature jumped at us, making us all drop on the floor. Then, it leaped over us and up – out of the mine. Phew! Then, we heard loud screams from Tup and Keith. The creature was perhaps a cross between a huge dog and a wolf. As we started to get back to reality, sitting up, I wondered what the heck was that. We started to recompose ourselves when we heard someone moan from down the mine. It sounded like Dickie. So, suddenly, the dog-like animal we had just seen was at the back of our memory, and we made swiftly made our way to Dickie. He was still half in and half out of the tub when it derailed and turned on its side. Willis rushed down to Dickie, who had started to come around and was rubbing his eyes.

Bent over him, Willis asked, "Are you okay, mate?"

"My eyesight's all blurry. I can only see you vaguely," he replied nervously.

John awoke in my head and said, "Stand back, Alan. I'll see if I can help." For ten minutes, he waved his hands back and forth over Dickie's eyes, but when asked, 'Is that better?' Dickie still couldn't see clearly. As he spoke, the lamp started to flash on and off as though it was about to go out.

Oh no, that's all we need, to be plunged into darkness,' we all started to panic. Suddenly, the lamp turned a pure gold colour. This again triggered John into action, and he wrapped his hands around the lamp. The lamp started to pulsate and moved towards Dickie, who put his hands over his eyes, and we heard an immediate "Wow, that's much better!" He sat up with a smile on his face. However, we couldn't smile for long as the tub struck the wall of the shaft, causing a large crack to appear. The crack quickly grew larger, accompanied by a massive crackling noise, as if an enormous eruption was building up. Recognising what was happening, we all managed to move further into the mine, but unfortunately, the roof collapsed on us.

As the dust settled in the mine, we started to check if everyone was ok, and we could see we were trapped in the mine. The fall had blocked our escape route. We would have to wait until they got us some help to dig us out. Holding the lamp up to the light,

I said, "Be quiet a minute; I can hear trickling water. I hope we're not going to get flooded before they can dig us out." Making my way towards the water, I saw that it was the orange water that ran into the Ingllee. I thought if we followed it, maybe it would lead us out of here.

It was a move of desperation, but we didn't have much choice. It was terrifying since there was total darkness except for the miner's lamp. Eventually,

we could see a large pipe with the orange water running through it. We ran to the pipe in sheer desperation and excitement paddling through the orange water. At last, we could see daylight. Oh yes, we came out in the field above the Ingllee, where we flopped down in the grass. It was sheer extercyto be out of there. After resting up, we made our way back up the field to the drift mine where Tup and Kieth were waiting, waving, jumping up and down in excitement and relief. As I reached home I hid the miner's lamp in the coal house; I didn't want any questions because there is something special about that lamp.

CHAPTER: 05
BACK TO GULIEMI FARM

Getting back to the Row, I didn't say anything to Mum and Dad about the episode. I would have been in trouble just to be at the mine. So, it was easier to act dumb.

"You look like a scruff. What have you been up to?" Mum queried.

"We went down the woods, and I fell in the stream." I lied.

"We will get the tin bath out of the coal shed and get you bathed," Mum replied. As we had no bathroom or toilet in the house, the toilet was across the big yard full of big hairy spiders and a newspaper torn up in bits stuck on a nail. It made your arse sore. You had to be desperate to go there. Meanwhile, I said I would get the bath out of the coal shed just in case Dad spotted the lamp. I put the bath in front of the fire while Mum put several saucepans of water on the gas stove and one on the fire. After the bath, I went to bed after a strenuous day. I was asleep in minutes.

While I was in a deep and absorbing sleep, I had a

dream that I was with John, driving a milk wagon out of Chesterfield. I was still holding my head where I had a lump. John told me that we were about half an hour away from the farm. Suddenly, there was a loud noise as the wagon went lopsided and the

wheel came off . We had to stop and check it out. We found that the wheel was shattered and we didn't know what to do. It was getting dark and it would be completely dark in an hour. The only option we had was to ride the horses back to the farm and come back tomorrow with a new wheel. So, after uncoupling the horses, we rode them back steadily. We arrived at the farm as it was getting

Knucky, who was there, took the horses, fed them, gave them water, and bedded them down to rest for the night.Explaining the situation to Dad, he said, "You would have to go to the wainwrights in town, take the wheel and wait for it to get repaired or get a new one. You will have to take the spare cart with Knucky and sort it. We have a more serious problem. We have had an offer from a mining company – a couple of dodgy characters wanting to buy the north fields to open a coal mine. The money's good, but they are our prime fields, and I don't want a lifestyle change; I have told them a definite no anyway."

By the time we got up, Knucky had arranged everything and was ready to go. John and I jumped on the back of the cart with the wheel to the Wainwrights, which is situated on the other side of town.

"Do you know the way to the Wainwrights, Knucky?" I asked.

"Yes, through Plover Woods," he replied. It was still early, so we just relaxed and enjoyed the ride through the woods. We stopped at the town centre at a pie stall and had a meat pie. It was yummy. At about dinnertime, we reached The Wainwrights. We knew Tom, who owned the yard. He was an Irishman and

was ok, but he liked a drink and should finish off as soon as possible to get to the Alehouse. "It will be a couple of hours, Sonny," he told us. So, we uncoupled the horse and took it down to the stream for a drink and some cooling down. The horse went into the stream and then we stripped off to join it while Knucky went off to find an alehouse for a couple of hours. When we returned to the Wainwrights, the wheel was repaired and Tom had put it on the cart. Still, there was no Knucky, so we had to go looking for him. We found him at the first Alehouse we went to, The Lord Nelson. He was in there singing his head off. We weren't allowed in, so we asked a man to fetch him out. The man came half-carrying Knucly, and as soon as he let go of him, Knuckly flopped to the floor.

He was a dead weight, and we couldn't carry him. John nipped off to the Wainwrights for a wheelbarrow while I gently slapped his face to try to wake him, but to no avail. As John returned with the wheelbarrow, we both lifted him on and kept taking turns until we got him back to the cart and dumped him like a sack of potatoes. He just lay there snoring. Jumping on the cart, we set off to find the wagon and refit the wheel. Getting into town was busy. There was some protest going off, so we slowly weaved our way through the protesters. It was mayhem, banners being waved about, and it was turning into a riot. One man then jumped onto our cart with a banner shouting Down with WIGS, no sooner after leaping on, he fell backwards with a thud and an 'Aaaahh'. He landed on the road with a banner. Getting out of the town to the countryside was like heaven. It was calm, peaceful, and quiet. All we could hear here was the peaceful twitter of birds and the nearby stream ripples as the water ran over the rocks and pebbles. At last, we arrived at the brokendown wagon, and since Knucky was still unconscious, we fitted the wheel. John said he would wait with the wagon while I went back with the cart and Knucky. Arriving at the farm, I managed to dump Knucky in the barn on a pile of straw, and Dad tied the horses to the back of the cart; we returned to the wagon. Where is John? We approached the wagon, but there was no John to be seen. We scoured the area yet we couldn't find him. It was a mystery. "John, where are you?!" I was shouting.

CHAPTER: 06
WHERE IS JOHN?

"John, John," I was shouting, "Where are you?"

Suddenly, I felt Mum's hand on my shoulder. She was shaking me, asking me to wake up.

"Wake up, Alan. You're having a bad dream," she nervously shook me. When I awoke, I was back in the Row.

"Why are you shouting John's name? You know he's not with us anymore," Mum said.

"I think he is, Mum. He's somewhere." I replied and then told her the stories, flashbacks, and dreams.

"It would have been nice, Alan, but he's not here, darling," Mum said, "When you were born, the nurse came and told me that only one had survived."

"Well, I know he's real. He's out there, somewhere." I argued.

Getting up and looking out of the back window that looks onto the allotments, I could see Tup and his mate Stalin (Stal) had taken over one of the plots that already had an old pigsty. They were carrying a crate with two baby piglets in it and I decided to go and have a closer look. I trotted downstairs and across the yard to the allotment where they were just putting the piglets in their new home. I asked them what they had named them, and Tup replied,

"Tom and Jerry".

I burst out laughing and said, "That's funny!" Tup then informed me that they were going to fence the area, keep 50 hens there, and call it "The Ranch".

"Wow, that will keep you busy," I said.

We had a chat and decided we would all meet in the British orchard to sort out the Bonfire. No matter what I did throughout that day, I couldn't get John out of my mind. It was so real. My mind kept flashing back to the dream, flashback, whatever you want to call it. I went over to the orchard to meet the lads, and we all went around the perimeter of the orchard trimming and cutting down trees for the Bonfire, but the picture in my mind kept coming back to me. It was like a house with a water mill on the side. The two guys that John had problems with yesterday were all mixed up in one. It was like a film on a loop that kept on rewinding and replaying. Getting back home in the Row, I went upstairs, laid on the bed, relaxed and tried to concentrate on John. I closed my eyes and then did some slow breathing exercises, saying, "Where are you?" Send me a message.

All I was getting was the image of the water Mill House then Plover wood. I remembered the miner's lamp in the coal shed that had magical properties. So, I went down the stairs quickly and entered the shed. The lamp was still there. I went back upstairs and put the lamp on the bed. I placed both of my hands around it and stared into the light. I closed my eyes, and suddenly, everything started spinning around me. I felt dizzy and terrified, and lights were flashing. There was a humming sound that grew louder and louder, humm, HUMMM, HUMMMM, then I blacked out.

When I came to, I was swirling through the air as though I was inside a large firework display. Suddenly, everything went quiet, and I found myself sitting in a wagon near Plover Wood at Guliemi Farm. However, there was still no sign of John. Just then, Dad came up to the wagon and said, "You wouldn't find John there, Alan."

"Dad, have you heard of a place, Water Mill House in Plover Wood? I think John has sent me a sign." I inquired.

Dad said, "I didn't tell you that the two men that came to buy the land warned me that if I didn't sell, something dreadful would happen. I'm afraid they might have kidnapped him."

So, Dad and I set off into the woods looking for the

Water Mill house. Dad said, "Let's follow the stream, and it should lead us to the house. After about half an hour, we spotted the house and lay low for a while to see any signs of life or sounds. Ten minutes later, two men came out of the house, shook hands and embraced each other, saying now he'll sell. As

they went around the back, we heard a horse and cart rattling its way off. They've gone. Slowly making our way to the house, we had a good look around and noticed that it was quiet inside. Although it was risky, we decided to break in and investigate. We kicked the door open and were immediately startled by the sound of someone moaning under the table.

they went around the back, we heard a horse and cart rattling its way off. They've gone. Slowly making our way to the house, we had a good look around and noticed that it was quiet inside. Although it was risky, we decided to break in and investigate. We kicked the door open and were immediately startled by the sound of someone moaning under the table. Upon further inspection, we discovered that it was John, who had been tied up. We quickly untied him and ran away like scared rabbits. As we made our way through the woods, we began to calm down, and we were almost at the wagon when we saw it. The horses were still there, tied to the wagon. We hopped on and rode towards town to report the incident to the Peelers. Once we arrived at the Peelers Station, my dad went inside to tell the story and report the men.

The Peelers said that they knew about the men and were already looking for them. A couple of con artists had tried similar things in this area. Driving back through town back through Plover wood, we were all on the edge, looking around in all directions. It wasn't until we approached Guliemi Farm that we started to calm down.

"Knucky!" shouted Dad, who usually slept in the barn.

"We have had trouble with a couple of men waiting there." He went into the house and came out with a Witworth rifle. Apparently, Knucky was a veteran of the Napoleonic wars with France and was handy when it came to the crunch. "Get in the barn for the night, get under the straw, and if any prowlers come poking their noses in our farm during the night, let them have it," Dad ordered.

So off we marched into the farmhouse. Dad went into the pantry and came out with another Witworth rifle. He lay down on the sofa, pulled his hat over his eyes and said, "Off to bed you two, leave this to me."

We lay in bed staring up at the ceiling for a couple of hours, jumping and twitching at every sound until tiredness and exhaustion took over. "Kerbang, kerbang" broke the silence. It was like two bombs going off. We all jumped up. Bill and Ben were first out of the door and hurried into the barn, barking like mad, until they suddenly went quiet.

By the time we arrived, Bill and Ben were laid by the side of two strange men who were writhing on the floor. Knucky had uncovered himself from under the straw. Apple of Straw said, "They were trying to steal the horses, so we let them have it, just to stop them running away. Blowing on the end of his Whitworth rifle, he added, 'I haven't lost my touch.' Dad then bound the men's hands, loaded them onto the back of the wagon, and he, along with Knucky, headed to the Peelers Station. Meanwhile, John and I, with arms around each other in brotherly affection, climbed into bed and fell into a deep sleep. Upon waking, I initially felt John's warmth, but as I opened my eyes, it was Sally, nuzzling me affectionately as if we hadn't seen each other for days, reminding me I was back in the Row.

CHAPTER: 07

TWO WORLDS INTO ONE

Sally was getting tucked into her doggy meat. Dad, Mum, and I were having breakfast, boiled eggs with toasted soldiers to dip in, when Uncle Urn walked in looking at me. He had come for the peelings and stuff we had saved, "What were you doing in Chesterfield yesterday, young fellow?" he asked me.

"I wasn't in Chesterfield yesterday, Pieclet," I answered. "You were, Teacake. I saw you at the market, and I shouted how yer going Teacake. You gave me such a look that I'd insulted you, then turned your back on me and walked away in disgust. Well, if it wasn't you, it was your double." He said.

I've had a feeling John was so near me for the last few weeks. It's like telepathy; he's so close yet so far away, I thought to myself. The rest of the day, I felt uneasy; I went up to watch Tup and Stal putting posts up and fencing for their ranch. They had 50 young hens coming in a couple of days and wanted to get it done. I then went over to the orchard, where there were a few of the lads bringing wood from everywhere for the bonfire, but I couldn't settle. All along, I thought John was just in my head, but now I have the feeling that those thoughts might have been telepathic messages all along and that he is somewhere in this world.

I have to go to Chesterfield after what Pieclet had told me. It was a long shot, but it was market day tomorrow, and I could sneak off, jump on the number 3 East Midland bus, and be there. I went up to bed with sheer excitement and anticipation. On entering the bedroom, I reached under the bed where I had hidden the miner's lamp and wondered if it could tell me anything. Lighting it up, I clasped it with both hands. Staring into the light, I kept repeating, where's John?

Where is my twin? However, nothing happened. Perhaps I'm wrong. Perhaps he is only in my head.

As I started to drift off, vague images began to emerge. It appeared to be a busy market, with noise and people milling around. But as quickly as it came, it disappeared. Was that all I would get as I fell asleep from sheer exhaustion? The night was long and restless, filled with tossing and turning. Suddenly, I woke up drenched in sweat, and another image appeared in my troubled mind. It was a foggy image again, but as the mist cleared, the number 27 came into view.

I had to think of an excuse to get out for a few hours

to catch number 3 to Chesterfield. So, over breakfast, I dropped it out that me and the gang were going down Eckington Woods for the day. OK, that was no problem. We're all set, I thought to myself.

"I'm buzzing. See you later, Mum," I shouted as I headed down to the Crown Corner bus stop. I jumped on the bus, and I was there in half an hour. I thought I'd have a look at the market first to see if anyone resembles him. I walked around the Market for about an hour, and I don't know what I was expecting, a miracle perhaps, then another hour walking around the town centre. Feeling really disheartened, I made my way to the bus terminus and got on number 3 back to Mosborough. I went upstairs feeling really fed up now. As the bus set off, someone caught my eye in the distance. Was it wishful thinking? Were my eyes playing tricks on me? No.

It can't be, is it? He looked like me. The bus was ready to turn the corner and I lost sight of the boy.

Come on, ALAN, make your mind up. Are you going or not?' I thought to myself, then sprang downstairs three steps at a time and got to the exit of the bus, but it was going so fast I couldn't jump off. Then, the bus slowed down to go around a corner, and I went for it. It felt as though I was in the air for minutes, but when I landed, I went arse over shit, did about ten roli-polies, but I sprang up like magic and set off running towards the street the boy was on. I reached the spot where the boy was, but he was nowhere to be seen. Oh no, I've lost him, bugger, I said to myself, I've blown it now. I might as well carry on down this street now, I said to myself. I'll walk down to the end of this street and then back towards the bus, I thought to myself. As I looked around, my eyes fell upon a row of shops. Suddenly, my attention was drawn to a sign that hung on the wall between two of the shops. It read "Upstairs Flat No. 27". The sight of it caused my heart to race with excitement and fear. I stood there for ten or fifteen minutes, unsure of what to do next. I was frozen in place.

I thought, it's now or never. What's the use of walking away now? With bated breath, I opened the door and started climbing up the stairs, one step at a time. Each step increased my apprehension and fear - fear of the unknown and fear of failure. But it was too late to turn back now. I knocked on the door, not knowing what I was going to say. The door opened, and a lady in her thirties stood there, staring at me in disbelief. She put her hand to her mouth and screamed, "No, no!" Then, as she collapsed, I looked into the room and saw myself – or rather, someone who looked just like me – sitting in a chair with his mouth hanging open in disbelief. It was John.

We just stood there looking at each other, not knowing what to say or do. It was like looking in a mirror. Both of us were dressed in similar black trousers, and my red top was identical to his brown top. I hesitantly walked slowly into the room, sitting down next to him. The lady was coming around sobbing to me, "I'm so sorry". I was looking at myself and then John saying I have been dreading this moment all my life.

"Who is this, Mom?" John whispered.

"This is your twin, Alan." She replied.

"What's happening mom?" As he spoke, I looked at the lady, and her face seemed familiar, then slowly, it all came back to me.

"When I took my first breath, I thought my lungs were going to burst, we have been together for nine months in our first world. Now we're here in this strange, noisy world. My first thought was, where is John? Where is my twin? I tried to look around for him. He was there struggling for breath in this new world, and I opened my eyes to see him take his last breath. Then to see this nurse, this lady taking him away."

"That's where I've seen you. You stole my brother. What happened?" The lady sat up and started sobbing. Between the sobs, she began explaining her story.

"When John had taken his last breath, I wheeled the unit out of the theatre. While going down the corridor, he started coughing and spluttering, so I quickly wheeled him into an empty private room. Then he opened his eyes and gave me such a lovely smile, I started to think, as I couldn't have a child of my own, this was my last chance. So, I took him home and brought him up as my own. I know it was wrong, but I couldn't resist him when he smiled at me."

Finishing her story, John looked at me with tears in his eyes and whispered, "Where is my real mum, Alan?"

"About six miles away," I answered.

As he was wiping tears away, he stood up and said, "Let's go then. I'm ten years late." We both stood up and walked away.
Getting down the steps and outside, I threw my arms around him and said, "I've missed you, brother." We marched to the bus terminus without saying a word, the bus trip did seem like a lifetime. Then suddenly, we were at Mosborough. Walking up High Street towards the row, people were just standing there looking but not believing what they were seeing.

Then, we reached No 17 Mosborough Moor. I got John to knock on the door, and as he knocked, I stood away out of sight, and Mum came to the door saying, "Come in, Alan.

What are you waiting for?"

Then, I jumped out shouting, "SURPRISE, SURPRISE."

CHAPTER: 08

THE HOMECOMING

Mum's face was suddenly drained of all blood as she covered her mouth with her hands, then jumped at John with her arm around him, sobbing, "My darling, how is this possible? Where, what, how?" Words wouldn't come out. Shaking and trembling from head to foot eventually stuttered, "I MUST BE DREAMING. It's not possible. You left us in grief and devastation." She let go of John for a moment, then sprang back into his arms as if he was about to disappear again, holding him like a coiled spring. I retorted with a half-laugh and a half-cry, "Hey, what about me? I'm in this family, too," to which she opened her arms to bring me into the fold. "Where's Dad?" I stammered all this emotion was starting to affect me.

"He is up at the allotment", Mum said while running to the door, screaming, "Arthur!" at the top of her voice.

Dad, strolling down from the allotment with a spade in one hand and a cabbage bigger than a football in the other, shouted, "Whatever the matter, love, calm down. You'll give yourself a heart attack."

I thought to myself Dad wouldn't rush even if the

was on fire, until he spotted both John and me together. Then, as though he was in a trance, he dropped the spade and the cabbage, which went rolling down the yard, coming to a halt between two clothesline posts and as it happened, he threw his arms in the air as if he had scored a goal. "He stood transfixed, then rubbed his eyes and let a teardrop fall. In a manly fashion, he brushed it aside and came running towards us. I mean, nobody ever saw Dad run. He put his strong arms around us and swung us around as though he was doing the Hokey Pokey. 'Wow, where have you been, young man, all my life?' he exclaimed before flopping down in a chair, as if he was having trouble comprehending the situation and then laying back in exhaustion.

Watch out for more adventures of ALAN & JOHN

In book three   DOUBLE- TROUBLE

CHAPTER: 09
DOG WOLF

The news of Jhn's arrival spread like fire in the village, and slowly, as the day went on, there was a steady stream of friends and neighbours to know what, where, when, and how this had happened.

As the sun gradually set, the group dispersed after hearing the story. Outside, we chatted in our small yard until it was completely dark. Suddenly, we heard a commotion from TUP and STALS Ranch, with hens squawking and flying in the air. My dad suspected that a fox had entered the ranch. As we approached, a large, dark creature quickly slinked away. Looking up, we saw a large animal silhouette against the moon in the distance on top of the allotments. I asked Dad, "What's that?"

"No clue. I haven't seen anything this large before. Sure, it's not a fox, at least." He replied. As we were chatting amongst ourselves, Sally shot off after it, like a bullet through the Hedges and undergrowth towards it. We were afraid for her and shouted for her to come back, but she wasn't listening. As Sally got closer to the animal, it didn't move. Then suddenly, we heard Sally whimper. We all rushed over to the hedges, but when we got there, there was nothing - no animal, no Sally. All was quiet as the grave and we couldn't find any trace of her.

We searched the undergrowth and surrounding fields for hours, calling out Sally's name, but to no avail. Eventually, we gave up and made our way back home with a heavy heart, knowing that Sally was still missing. As we stood in the bedroom window, looking out over the allotment, we saw the animal thing reappear, howling away in a mocking gesture. We got into bed with our hands over our ears to shut out the haunting sounds, eventually giving in to the darkness and the restlessness feeling of fear and nightmares that was enveloping us.

Just as it was becoming daylight, John suddenly

suddenly jumped up in bed and nudged me. He picked up the Miners Lamp from under the bed and whispered, "What's this for?"

"It helped me find a mate that was lost, and I think it might have magical properties," I replied.

"Well, then, I think it might help us in finding Sally," John suggested. "What do you have to do with it then?"

"Well, we have to put our hands on and concentrate. Let's give it a try!" I said. So we both put our hands on the lamp and it started to change colour and flash about. Then, as the colours faded, Alan and John could both see blackness, but with Sally visible in the darkness.

"That's not much help," John frustratingly stated.

"Oh yes, it is," I said as I tapped him on the shoulder and smiled. "I've come across something like the dog-wolf before. It was down an old drift mine across the road." Let's go and look," John impulsively suggested.

"What's up, Al? You scared?"

Trying to hide my fears, I stated, "Of course not, John. Let's go before Mom and Dad wake up. Bring the lamp." We quickly got dressed, out of the house, across the road, and down to the mine."

"Look down there," said John, pointing towards the mine shaft.

"Look down there," said John, pointing towards the mine shaft.

"That's where I saw something similar to a dog or a wolf," I replied.

Without any fear or hesitation, he marched down the drift mine, shouting, "One on, Al! We need the lamp."

My heart was racing, but John showed no signs of

fear as we made our way down. We had not gone a couple of hundred yards when two large yellow eyes appeared out of the darkness. "What the flaming heck is that?" John suddenly showed he was human after all, stopping dead in his tracks.

We were startled by a loud growl, causing us to step back a few yards. Sally came running towards us from the darkness, but we could still see the two yellow eyes. We quickly retreated from the mine with Sally, and when I looked at John, his face was drained of blood, and terror was in his eyes. I started laughing, perhaps out of fear and relief. We marched back down Bramalls Lane and into number 17. As we heard the door shut, Dad came downstairs and bent over to greet Sally, who was licking him all over. He asked her where she had been, and we examined her for injuries, but she was unharmed. We found her at the door and lied to Mum, saying we were just making noise while coming back upstairs. Mum was relieved to see Sally and asked where she had been. We didn't know, but we were happy that she was okay. We all went back to bed for a few more hours.

The next morning, we had boiled eggs from my banty hens and toast for breakfast. John and I decided to go out and explore the village and meet people. We went to the allotment first and saw Uncle Urn (Pieclet). He looked at me and then, not knowing who was who said, "How yer doing, Teacake?" to which I replied, "Ok."

Piecet then looked at me and said, "Oh, you're Alan, patting John on the head and said pleased to meet you, sonny Jim. I'm just feeding the pigs there, getting ready for market soon,

I pointed at the pigs whom I had nicknamed Doris

and Doreen. "Who is putting on weight now?" I asked.

"Market," Pieclet replied.

"What do you mean, market? They are my friends, those two! You can't do that," I pleaded with him.

"I have to. They are worth a lot of money. That's the whole point of it. That's life," he said, walking away and shrugging his shoulders."

Next, we went up to Tup and Stalin's Ranch. Reaching the ranch, I shouted, "Hi, you two! This is my brother, John." "Yer so I heard," he said without looking up, sounding disinterested. He told us the 'bloody fox' has been attackng a couple of hens and had done some damage. It dug a hole under the fence, took two hens, and frightened the others. They will not be laying eggs now until they settle down. It will cost us a fortune as we have to keep selling eggs to pay for the feed. They even frightened Tom and Jerry, as Tup called them.

"That wasn't no fox," I said.

"Of course, it was. What else could do that damage?" Stal snarled, sounding fed up with it all.

"It was bigger than a fox, more like a giant dog wolf," John replied.

Tup walked into the sty to feed Tom and Jerry, laughing to himself.

"Listen, lads, I need a favour," I said. "Uncle Urn is going to take Doris and Doreen to market soon, and they are like two friends to me. If we can take Tom and Jerry down to mate them, it would save their lives if we can get them preggers.

"Ok," Stal said, "As we're struggling, let's say a Fiver a pig, so you will owe us

£10."

"Uncle Urn has gone to the pub, so now's the time," I said.

"Ok, let's do it. Should be a laugh," Stal proceeded to get some rope out of the sty, tying it around Tom and then Jerry. It was like taking two dogs on leads for a walk; it looked right funny. So, we all went laughing all the way down to Pieclets pig sty. On our way down, we bumped into my Dad's friend Albert {horsey} Large.

"Where are you gang going, Alan?" Horsey shouted.

"We're just taking Tom and Jerry for a walk." We walked away, laughing. On reaching Peiclet's sty, we led them in to meet Doris and Doreen. So to speak, it was quite funny watching Tom and Jerry getting acquainted with Doris and Doreen – if you know what I mean; we stood laughing our heads off. When they had finished getting acquainted, Tup and Stal led the pigs away, patting them on the back, saying, "Well done, lads. We are proud of you. You're going to be daddies soon." Turning around to us, they shouted, "You owe us £10."

CHAPTER: 10
GULEIMI

That afternoon we went across to the spare land across from the British Oak, where most of the lads met next to Mic and Tony Havenhand, who were the only ones in the village with a TV. As it was the Queen's coronation coming tomorrow, I wanted to see if there was any chance of gate crashing to watch it.

Getting there, we went around the lads, introducing my twin,

John. There was Mic and Toni, Keith and Tich, and the Wainwright cousins. They were all pleased to meet John, whom they had heard about through the grapevine, but were still surprised at how identical we were. They were discussing a large dog-like animal that had been ravaging hens, geese and small lambs on Woolleys farm, and the Woolleys have been out with their shotguns, looking for the beast.

While we were all talking, I could hear a little cheep, cheep, coming from under the hedge. Moving over towards the noise, I bent down to look, and there was a small baby Jackdaw. It looked as though it had dropped out of a tree somewhere because they only nest in trees, then got lost, wondering about looking for Mum. We all had a good look around, but we couldn't see where it had fallen from. Eventually, I decided to take it and put it in my banty hen house. So, John and I set off back to the row up to where my banty hens were. There, we picked up a nesting box, fastened it high up so the hens couldn't get it, gave it a few worms and I thought we would try to rear it. We collected four eggs while I was there, fed the hens and locked them up until morning.

Getting back home, we went up into the bedroom to relax, and while we were there, John started to look around the bedroom and picked up a box from under the bed. "Do you mind if I have a nosy?" he asked.

"No," I said, "Help yourself." After scrounging around in the box, he came out with a scroll of old parchment rolled up and tied. Unwrapping it, he looked at it and asked what's this. I had forgotten all about it. It was the scroll Guleimi gave me.

So I told John the whole story of going down the Iglelee woods with Ray Garfit, finding the healer Guleimi, who travelled forward in time from 1822 to the present times only at certain times to heal animals, and him telling me that I was his 7th grandson, and so he was passing on to me the healing powers and the scroll.

I was only seven at the time and have not seen much of healing powers only when you came into my mind and took over (telling John).

"Do you think we can find him again?" John pleaded with me to sort this healing thing out.

"I can't think how we can call him back," I replied.

"What if we go to the spot in the woods with the miner's lamp and see if we can call him back with the lamp?" John asked.

"I'll tell you what; we will go down tomorrow and give it a try," I said to shut him up about it.

The next morning, after breakfast, we went up to our hen house to feed the banties Jack the Jackdaw, digging him some worms and surprisingly, he was hopping. The banty hens had taken to him as one of their own. Sally was wondering around the allotment, and we weren't taking much notice until we heard a frightening growling noise coming from the hedges. As we looked up, we saw a dark, slinking figure under the hedge. It was a dogwolf staring at Sally. Quickly locking up the hen house to keep them safe, we picked up two large sticks and carefully went to get Sally on the lead to safety. Coming down from the allotment, we bumped into Uncle Urn.

"I'm baffled, teacake," he said, looking at me and then John, not knowing which one he was talking to. "I think Doris and Doreen are pregnant. I don't know how, but the teats are growing, and that's the first sign."

Smiling to myself, I said, "I think Tup's pigs, Tom and Jerry, have been on the loose."

As we walked away, John mentioned that we were going down Inglee Woods to look for Guleimi. I had forgotten it was the Queen's Coronation today, and we said we would meet up at Micks's. We went across the road and into Micks. It was heaving, about 40-50 pushing and shoving to watch a TV of about 6 inches square only. We did not have much choice as Micks was the only one in the village with a TV. After a couple of hours, everybody started to drift away. Although, it was pretty impressive stuff in history and all that, it was a bit like watching paint dry. Going out of the house, we heard a shout

"HOY. You two owe us £10 for the pig caper," Tup shouted.

I retorted, "We have only got £3," I said.

"Well, we've had a couple of hens taken by that Dog-wolf thing, so do us a favour and get yourself over to see if you can buy a couple of chickens of Brian Wooley." He replied.

It was too late in the day to go down Inglee, so we thought it was a nice walk. Let's get off.

We had a lovely walk to Wooley's Farm. We went up to the bridle path, down into the woods, which we call The Jungle, and across a cornfield. As we entered the farm, we were greeted by several large geese that started running towards us aggressively. Sally was scared and ran back across the cornfield and out of sight. We were about to follow her when Brian Woolley came out and shooed the geese away. He looked at me and John and said, "This looks like double trouble."

"Can I help you, lads?" he asked.

"We're here to buy a couple of chickens if possible," I nervously stutted with one eye on the geese. "How much you got, sonny?" he asked.

"£3," I replied.

"Well, they are £2 each. You can have one and a half," he said, laughing out loud at his own joke. "I'll tell you what, because you're Arthur's lads, I'll sell you two for £3."

"Thanks, Brian. You're a star." As I was speaking, I could see the dog-wolf from the corner of my eye in one of those dogpound vans. "How have you caught him?" I asked, pointing at the dog-wolf thing.

"Well, he's been after our hens and lambs, so we put out some meat with sleeping tablets in and found him snoring fast asleep under a hedge. Then, we sent for the dog-pound van, and they will keep him in the dog-pound up Queen Street until they can find a zoo that will have him." Brian said, putting the two chicks in the little fishing basket.

Striding off with a spring in our step, pleased with the result and it will keep Tup and Stal quiet, Sally came to meet us now the geese were out of sight. She wasn't keen on them geese; they were too big and noisy. Getting back to the ranch, we handed the chickens over, and the job was sorted. Then, off we went to feed Jack and the banty hens. Jack was strutting around the coit as though he was one of the girls. The hens had taken to him as though he was their own; he was growing and developing his feathers, and I suppose soon he would want to fly off. I hope not because I have been told you can learn Jackdaw to talk like a parrot. We started off learning to talk curve with {How yer doing Jack}, but he just cocked his head to one side, looking at us as if he was puzzled. After five minutes of this speech therapy, we gave it up as a bad job [perhaps when he's a bit older, we could try again if he's still here, we thought]. Then, collecting four eggs, we locked up and made our way down to the Row.

Getting back to number 17, Dad made an announcement. I think Sally is going to be a mummy, in fact, I'm sure. I don't know when and how, but you two haven't been looking after her properly. Anyway, what's done is done, and we will have to wait to see what colour, shape or breed they will turn out to be.

"That's brilliant news, Dad!" We both chirped up at once, with a big smirk on our faces. Then, putting radio Luxemburg on the radio, we sat back to listen to the new Top 20 show of music.

CHAPTER: 11
GULEIMI

Getting in bed, John chirped up, "Are we going down the Inglee wood tomorrow?"

"Yes, I promise. We will go and look for Guliemi, although I doubt we will find him. He is not the person you can make an appointment to see, I had forgotten all about him until you found the scroll. If he had turned up that often, everybody would have seen him."

The sun woke us up, beaming through the window. Looking out, it looked busy on the allotments. Dad was up there digging. Next to him was Albert (horsey) Large, then Tup and Stal repairing fencing and Uncle Urn (Pieclet) feeding the soon-to-be moms pigs Doris and Doreen.

After breakfast, John, Sally and I set off for Inglelee Woods with, of course, the miner's lamp. It was a sunny day, and as we entered the woods, we were struck by the beauty of the bluebells. Sally was busy chasing squirrels up the trees and rabbits down the holes.

We started at the top of the woods, following the Orange water. We walked towards the bottom of the woods, looking left and right, but there were no signs of Guleimi. I said to John, "We're wasting our time doing this because he only comes occasionally, in the last 200 years, and we don't know if and when he will appear. I think me and Ray just got lucky."

John said, "Ok, let's try the lamp, then work our way back up the wood, and if we don't come across him, we will abandon the idea for today and go home."

We sat down on the grass with our hands around the lamp, concentrating. The lamp was flashing on and off as though something was going to happen while Sally was cocking her head to one side and wondering what we were up to. Suddenly, there was a loud crack and bang. Then, lights of every colour came spinning out of the lamp as we jumped back away from the lamp in shock. It was like a bonfire night, but the lights went away and subsided. We looked around; we were sure something had triggered, but no, everything went quiet and back to normal as we looked at each other, shrugging our shoulders in resignation. "Let's go home, Al," said John. We slowly bowed our heads in sadness and started trudging our way back up to the woods. Sally walking in the orange water, started barking at the fresh air, running around in circles and going berserk.

"What's up, girl?" John shouted to her, and as we turned the corner, there was a huge roar then standing on a large rock was what looked like the wolfdog, surrounded by a mist and as cleared-it can't be, we saw it locked up, but it was the wolfdog.

Shaking with fear, we backed off as we heard a gentle voice saying, "Abel down, boy," turning the corner, there was a man-like tramp sitting with his feet bathing them in the orange water.

"GULEIMI," I shouted, looking at him and then John in disbelief.

"Alan and John," he said quietly, "I wondered how long it would take for you two to find each other. But I knew you would."

We couldn't take our eyes off the wolfdog. "I thought he had been captured," I said.

"No," Guleimi answered. "That would be his bad

brother, Cain. Abel is the nice one of the twin wolfdogs." We started to relax as he spoke, glancing at a bright twinkling stone around his neck. I looked at John; he was transfixed and couldn't take his eyes off it.

"What's that?" John quizzingly uttered.

"I'm glad you have asked that," Guliemi replied, "That's why I've returned from my past to pass on this knowledge, this gift to you two. What's so special about it is we both churned in at the same time. Nobody knows the secret until you come into contact with it. It has a different effect on every person, that's why it can be a gift, or a curse that's why it has to be kept secret. You can never tell until it makes contact with your body."

Explaining the story of the stone, Guleimi explained, "About 250 years ago, I was a young lad in these same woods Inglelee. The name is an old Saxon name meaning hanging lee. I knew these woods like the back of my hand until one day, I came across a rock face at the deepest part of the woods that I had seen many times before, but this time was different. Watching the Orange Water trickle into a small crack in the rock face, I investigated further, moving bushes and brambles aside. There was an opening, just large enough for a small boy to squeeze through. It was dark in there and waist-deep in water. Dare I investigate, I thought to myself. Slowly, cautiously, I edged my way into the water. It was getting deeper now up to my chest. Trembling, something drove me on into the darkness. The water was getting more shallow now. I had gone about fifty yards when I saw the light; things were getting brighter and brighter. Suddenly, I was in a vast, colourful cavern. What caught my eye was a small blue Johnstone brighter than anything in the world. Getting out my knife, I prodded it off the face of the cavern. Immediately grasping the stone, I felt a calmness and serenity about myself, and as time went on, I discovered it had given me this gift to heal animals, amongst other gifts that I discovered in time, but beware, if you seek this gift it could also be a curse.

This is not just an ordinary Blue John; it is called Bluest Blue John and it is a rare form with magic properties, but it can take many forms of magic, including Black Magic. Different people react to the stone in different ways, and you never know how it will affect you until you handle it.

"How do we get some then?" John piped up. Guleimi explained you have to follow the Orange Water down the woods to a large Oak tree. There is one branch that is like finger-pointing the morning after a full moon at sunrise exactly, and as the sun hits the tree dawn, a sunbeam will point the way to the rock face. You might not see the rock face at first. It's covered with bushes and brambles, which you have to clear out of the way to reveal a small opening that leads to a large cavern.

"Cavern, cavern," his voice echoed and as he uttered the words, a blue mist appeared from nowhere and enveloped him. As his words echoed ever silently, he was gone with the mist, leaving only the evidence of the recent activities. Abel, the Wolfdog, glanced around as though he was looking for Gulieimi and shot off like the wind. We sat there as if in a daze.

"I've never seen anything like that," John said, scratching his head in bewilderment. "Did that actually happen, or was I dreaming?"

"Well, that was what we were looking for, and we did get to see him. We will have to wait till the next full moon and come back down to follow his guidance." I said. Meanwhile, Sally was smelling around the area where Abel had been, "Come on, girl," I shouted to her, but she was struggling to walk, walking a few steps and then collapsing on the floor. We started to panic, "Let's pick her up and take her home," John said as she was whimpering quietly to herself. I carefully picked her up, and we took turns carrying her home.

Getting back to number 17, we shouted to Dad, "Something's wrong with Sally." We put her down on the carpet, and Dad came running in. As he bent down to examine her, he said smilingly, "She's about to have pups."

We were all the more relaxed now, and Dad made her a bed under the cupboard near the sink, saying, "You have to leave her now to get on with it. She wants peace and quiet, and don't disturb her. Go and check on the banty hens and your jackdaw and see if there are any eggs for our tea."

We brought a spade with us to dig up some worms for Jack. As soon as we opened the door, Jack flew out and settled in a nearby tree. We were amazed that he could fly and worried that we might not be able to get him back. John looked at me with a frown and suggested we dig up some worms to lure him back. We found some small worms and put them on the staging while calling out, "Come on, Jack." To our surprise, Jack flew down and started gulping down the worms. He looked at us and said, "Come on, Jack." We both burst out laughing as we had never heard a Jackdaw talk before. We tried to test him out by saying, "Good boy, Jack," and he repeated it back to us. It made our day. We put him to bed, collected four eggs, locked up the coit, and went down for our tea.

As we entered the house, Mum called out, "Boys, Sally has given birth to just one pup. It's a miniature version of her. It looks like she's only having one this time." Excitedly, we rushed in to take a quick look and then left her alone. Dad warned us not to disturb her until tomorrow.

Later, during tea, I asked Dad to check his diary and tell me when the next full moon would be. "Why do you want to know?" he asked, pulling out his diary. Glancing at John, I quickly lied and said, "Oh, there's supposed to be a meteor shower early that morning."

After scanning his diary, he replied, "Tomorrow night is the full moon. But you won't get me out of bed for that. You're welcome to it." I began to get excited, thinking about the cavern and the Blue John. We would have to wake up at 5 AM to get to the woods and find the cavern before sunrise. However, we had all day tomorrow to plan everything out.

The next morning, we couldn't wait to go down and see little Sally Junior. Dad said as long as we are careful and don't touch Sally or the pup, we can

have a quick look. Quietly sneaking downstairs, both of us pulled back the curtain that Dad had rigged up to give Sally a bit of privacy. We could not believe our eyes, as well as little Sally Junior was all I could describe as a small baby bear, a little black fluffy thing.

"Where's that come from?" John said.

"Where do you think?" I said, laughing.

"I know, I mean, who is the Dad?" John asked.

"I think it's obvious it could only be wolf-dog. Let's hope it's Abel, not Cain." We better shout to Mum and Dad.

As we spoke, Mum and Dad came down, saying "What's the fuss?"

"You will never guess. We've got what looks like a baby bear." I replied. All four of us stood speechless. It looks odd, like a cuckoo in the nest; that pup is from Wolfdog.

Dad stated, "Well, at least he has a name. We might as well call him Bear." Dad closed the curtains and said leave them alone now. "Down at number 11, a new family is moving in. I've seen the man looks like a dodgy character," Dad said, "He's got guns, fishing tackle, hunting dogs, and ferrets. I bumped into him last night; he had a bag of turnips and asked if I wanted to buy any turnips. I said no thanks, and he said, 'You wouldn't believe it, the farmer left them out all night, so I have taken some of them (nudge, wink, wink), know what I mean?' so I just gave him a funny look and walked away, but what might interest you they have a girl about your age."

John's ears sprang up. "Now you're talking, Dad," he said.

"What's she like?" I enquired. Quite pretty was his reply.

"Shall we have a mozy down there and suss them out?" John nudged me and gave a wink, "Come on, Al."

Getting down to number 11, this guy was sitting outside in an old armchair. He was chewing a matchstick in his mouth, with a gypsy-like scarf thing round his neck and a flat cap pulled over to one side, wearing it like a beret. "Mornin' lads, how yer doing?

I've just got the very thing for you two. Bloomin heck, I'm seeing double. I bet you two are a handful. Double trouble, I think," he then nudged and winked, then said, "Only kidding, lads digging me in the ribs with his elbow."

This guy never stops, I thought, as he pulled a bag of jewellery out of his pocket, took out a couple of rings, saying the solid gold special price for you two fiver each, let's hav yer.

Crickey John said to me, "Does this guy come up for air?"
Then, he turned towards the man and said, "No, thank you, Sir."

On hearing John calling him a sir laughed his head off for about ten minutes, nearly choking but managing to spit it out.
"That's a good un, Sir. That's the last thing still chewing on his matchsticks say that's a good un."
Then, shouting at the top of his voice, he said, "JULIA, bring us a cuppa, my luv, that's a good lass."

A blonde head appeared at the door and said, "Will do, dad." John flashed me a smile that said it all – she was certainly a looker.

I said, "We should be going now. We have to take care of the hens and feed Jack."

The man replied, "Nice to meet you lads, my name is Johnny Allsop. You should come round for tea sometime. I caught some rabbits this morning."

I declined his offer, saying that we already had our tea arranged. As we walked away, I whispered to John that I couldn't eat a rabbit because they were too cute and fluffy. John silently agreed.

We opened the hen coop and dug up some worms for Jack. He flew around for a bit and then settled on the decking. We tried to teach him some more English by saying "Morning Jack" repeatedly, but he just kept repeating it back to us. After getting bored, we collected the eggs and closed up the coop.

T6.

On our way back down, we bumped into Uncle Urn, "Morning teacake," he said, looking at me and then John not knowing who was who. "I've had some good news, Teacake. Doris and Dora have become mummies; they have two piglets each. I don't know how or when, but it's there for all to see. Do you want a look?"

Taking us into the sty, he said, "Now I've six pigs, and I've decided to start breeding and selling them off, so I will need an extension to this sty as I will be running out of room as the pigs get bigger, so there's a lot of work building with the sty and feeding the pigs. I'm wondering if you two want to help me, and I will give you 10% each of all the sales of baby pigs.

John said, "Make it 15% each, Pieclit, and you have a deal on one condition. You don't send Doris and Dora to market; you keep them for breeding."

So we shook hands on this, and we were in business. Pieclit said we would sell two of the baby pigs and keep two for breading as well. "Now, lads, we will need plenty of food for pig swill, oh and some timber for the extension." Said Pieclit.

"Ok, we're on to it," I said. We first went to see all the families in the row to save spare veg and stuff for pig swill. The next job was to get some large timber for the extension. That will have to wait because we have to plan for tomorrow to get Blue John.

Tomorrow, we will need a bag. We might as well get what we can of this Blue John; you never know, we might be able to sell some. Then we need a small pick, Dad's got one in the coal shed, a torch and our magic miner's lamp.

The next morning, we were up sharp at about 5 AM. It was just getting light the birds were whistling, and it looked like it was going to be a nice sunny day. So off we went after sneaking out of the house, across the road down Bramall Lane past mine and down the fields we were in the Inglee Woods. Following the Orange Water down, looking for the large Oak tree, it was very eerie in there. It wasn't quite light yet, and we were a bit on edge, nearing the bottom of the wood at last the Oaktree.

We sat under the tree, waiting for the sun to come up like Guleimi said. Those five minutes seemed like an hour. Then, eventually, a sunbeam shot through the tree like magic, pointing at a large branch to the right that pointed the way through dense undergrowth brambles, nettles and large ferns. I thought no wonder no one found this cavern. Then, we could see some large rocks moving the undergrowth to one side. Sure enough, there was a small opening. Climbing through the small aperture, we were thigh-deep in water straight away. I had a torch and a bag, and John had the miner's lamp on and the small pick axe. As we went further in, it got darker, and I was shaking with fear and trepidation. John had a worried look on his face, and the water was now up to our waist.

"Shall we go back, John?" I tapped him on the shoulder as I spoke.

"Wait a minute, I can see a chink of light," Joun replied.

"Wow I hope you're right. I have just about had enough," I said. Then, the light in the cavern hit us in all its magnificence. It was massive. We just stood there and admired the works of Mother Nature. We had never seen anything like it. When we got our breaths back, we started to look around for the Blue John, shining my torch on the walls. John was examining the other walls with the miner's lamp.

Holding the lamp up, I said, "Pass me the lamp for a minute, and as both our hands met together on the lamp, there was like an explosion of light that lit up the Blue John in the walls that had until now been invisible without the magic of the lamp.

I held the lamp up while John went to work, chipping

away and filling up the sack. It took us about an hour until the small sack was full.

"Let's go now before the water rises and we're stuck in here."

We were excited as we waded through the water, making our way back down the tunnel and out of the small entrance. The sun was now blazing hot, with its beams shining through the trees. It was a wonderful sight, especially after being in the cavern for so long. We had our rewards and were ready to enjoy the sunshine. It was around 8 AM, and if we were lucky, we might get back home before Mum and Dad woke up.

As we reached the row, we went up to the hen house with the sack of Blue John and hid it underneath. Job done. We then went into number 17, and all was still quiet. We sat and had a look at the dogs, knowing they would never know we had been out.

CHAPTER: 12
IN BUSINESS

Wasting no time after breakfast, we went down to the village and up Queen Street, where there was an old, retired jeweller, Tommy Bingley, who still did a bit of work on the side as a hobby more than anything. We picked two lumps of Blue John to craft and drill to make a necklace like Guleimi's, and then we will see its healing properties or see if it triggered any effect on us, as Guleimi had guaranteed. Sometimes, it could take several days to see any results.

Tommy's workshop was located at the back of his house, which was a small timber building. As we knocked on the door, a creaky old voice said, "Yes, come in." When we entered the little workshop, Tommy did not look up and continued with his intricate work. He then asked, "Yes, what can I do for you two fellow me lads?" Eventually looking up and lifting his small spectacles with a big friendly smile, Tommy was well known for his gentle and friendly manner. He was well-loved in the community because nothing was too much trouble for him.

We nervously started to explain that we had come across these two lumps of Blue John and wanted them tidied up and a hole drilled in to make a necklace each. "Not a problem for you two young whippersnappers," he chirped up, put them on the bench and said, "Come back tomorrow about dinner time and have a nice little pendant each for lads. Now be off with you and let me get on with my work," again not looking up as if were not there.

Then, we went up to our hen coop to check on Jack and the hens. We opened the door, and Jack flew out. He didn't go onto the tree as he usually did but instead flew away into the distance.

I said sadly, "I think we might have lost him for good now. We'll miss him." So, we proceeded to clean out the hen hut and feed them. We collected the eggs, and as we were about to lock up, Jack came flying back into the coop with something sparkling in his mouth. He went straight to his nest and dropped something down there. We went to investigate, and we couldn't believe our eyes. There were several gold rings, earrings, and other pieces of jewellery. Jack must have been collecting them for quite a while.

John shouted out, "Where have you been, Jack?" to which he replied, "Morning, Jack. Where have you been, Jack?" several times before shouting up. We looked at each other, and John said, "We've got a virtual gold mine in this bird. I'm sure Tommy Bingley will be interested tomorrow. What a day!"

We were up like the lark the next morning, excited about the day ahead. We opened up the banty hen house, fed the banties and Jack, and collected the jewellery from Jack.

"Thank you, Jack." John shouted to him and he replied with, "Thank you, Jack," back to us.

With a spring in our step, we marched down High Street, up Queen Street and up to Tommy Bingley's.

Through the gate into the backyard, we could see Tommy working away at the bench. We gave him a knock out of politeness, and he shouted, "Come in lads," but as we entered and he looked up, he looked twenty years younger. His grey hair had turned a lovely dark brown, his back was straight, and his wrinkles had almost disappeared.

"You look well, Tommy," John remarked.

"Do you know I feel as well as I haven't in years today. It's like a miracle."

John and I looked at each other with wonderment, recalling Guliemi's words that continuous contact with the Bluest John will have a different effect on every person.

"I've got something for you two!" he exclaimed, pulling out a small bag from a drawer. He was as excited as a father giving out Christmas presents, with a gleam in his eyes. "I have a feeling there's something special about these. I've felt a power like never before." He opened the bag to reveal two polished and honed Blue John stones, tied together with twine that looked out of place holding such precious gems. The stones were throbbing and sparkling with a strange energy, and they seemed almost alive.

"Who is having which?" he asked excitedly as if he knew some secret. The look in his eyes showed that he knew there was something special about them. He rubbed his hands together eagerly as if he couldn't wait for our reaction.

"I'll have this," John jumped in, snatching one of the stones from Tommy and putting it around his neck in anticipation. He was so shocked and bewildered when nothing happened. So I put the other one around my neck and immediately felt a calmness in mind and body that is hard to explain but a feeling of fulfilment in mind and body, a feeling of serenity, love and gratitude for all living things.

"I will give you two a bit of advice," Tommy said wisely, nodding his head as if he knew more than us. "I don't know what you two are up to. It worries me if you have to wear those stones, keep them out of people's view and wear them with stones on your back and not on your throat where people can't see them. There is something dangerously special about them, and the unpredictable prolonged visual effect they will have on others beware."

On hearing his advice, we both grabbed the stones and spun them around onto our backs. John was now looking nervous and agitated. "You alright, John?" I asked worryingly.

"I feel I bit weird. I'll be alright in a bit," John smeared back at me, "Mind your own business," with a snarl of anger I've never seen before on his face.

"How much do we owe you for the necklaces?" I asked Tommy.

"£10 for my time, sunny Jim," he said light-heartedly.

"I am afraid we haven't got the cash, but what we have is this," I said while pulling a selection of the jewellery out of my pocket. Amongst them was a ring. Seeing the ring, Tommy's eyes shot out of his head as if he had spotted the crown jewels. "Where did you get that ring from, you rascals?" He said while pointing at a small gold ring with a red stone in it.

I could have lied or made up a story, but Tommy was a straight guy who was ok with us, so I decided to tell him the truth, "It was Jack who brought it to us."

"Who the hell is Jack?" he quizzingly asked, scratching his head, puzzled.

"It's our pet, Jackdaw, he came back with it in his mouth,"

John shouted back angrily at Tommy with his eyes red with uncontrolled rage "What's it got to do with you?" He prodded Tommy several times in the chest, staring at the old man with obvious hatred. Tommy dropped down into his chair, shellshocked and started trembling with fear as John continued prodding him, shouting and screaming in uncontrolled rage.

"JOHN!" I grabbed him by the collar. "What's gotten into you?" I could not believe his reaction. John pushed me aside and, with his head in his hands, ran out of Tommy's cabin.

Running after John up to the top of Queen Street,

I caught up with him on the outskirts of the woods, sitting under a large oak tree with his head still in his hands, sobbing as I approached him. He looked up at me with eyes full of remorse, and I bent over him, carefully lifting the blue john from around his neck and replacing it with mine, then putting his around my neck as I tensed up, then waiting for a bad reaction. Instead, I felt a feeling of utter calmness and tranquillity. With relief, I looked down at John to see his reaction as he smiled, looked up at me, and then jumped up as if he were sitting on a bomb! With his hands around me, he said, "Sorry, Al."

"I think we better go back and apologise to Tommy." John came on, so we went back into Tommy's workshop.

John, with his head down, made his apologies, saying we would be back with the £10. As we were going out, Tommy added, You better take that jewellery up to Lord Daysbough at Mosborough Hall, where your Jackdaw pinched it from."

Approaching Mosborough Hall, I said to John, "How are we going to explain this?"

"Leave it to me. I've an idea." He replied.

There I stood with much trepidation, shaking in my shoes, not knowing what John had in mind. We walked up the drive through the colourful gardens. We felt as though we were in an alien world. I rang the bell, and a smart butler-like man answered the door. I stepped back, saying to John, "Here you go, it's all yours."

"Good morning, young men. What can I help you with?" he said, looking down over his glasses at us.

John replied, "We've found some jewellery, and we believe it belongs here, or so we've been told." John opened his hand, showing him the jewellery. The butler-type man jumped back as though he had an electric shock.

"My gosh, where the blooming heck have you got these from? Wait a moment!" He disappeared back into the hall, shouting, "My Lord, My Lord!"

Then appeared another man in a smart dressing gown with a cigarette in one hand and a large glass of something resembling brandy in the other hand. He looked down at the jewellery in John's hand, "My word, young men, where have you found these?"

John started stuttering, reminding me of Ray, "We..we..we were bird nesting, looking for jackdaw eggs and they. We're inside the nest," John looked up with a hopeful 'please believe me' look on his face.

Lord Daybough then pulled out of his pocket two large white five-pound notes and gave them to us as a gesture to thank us. He then said, "Now be off with you, you little rascals. I Believe you thousands wouldn't slam the door in our face."

After popping back to Tommy's to pay him the Ten pounds, we walked back to the Row. Getting into Row, as we walked past the new guy's house, Johnny Allsop, his daughter JULIA, came out and, seeing John, made a beeline for him, grabbed his hand, looked into his eyes, and said, "How her doing, John?"

Feeling really down and a bit jealous, I walked away when Julia shouted, "Hey Alan, have you met my twin sister, JANICE?"

THE END

Not really; it's just the beginning.

www.ingramcontent.com/pod-product-compliance
Lightning Source LLC
Chambersburg PA
CBHW072056110526
44590CB00018B/3196